Purim

Story and pictures by **Miriam Nerlove**

ALBERT WHITMAN & COMPANY
MORTON GROVE, ILLINOIS

For Aunt Ruth, with love.

ALSO BY MIRIAM NERLOVE

Christmas

Easter

Halloween

Hanukkah

If All the World Were Paper

Passover

Thanksgiving

Valentine's Day

Text and illustrations © 1992 by Miriam Nerlove.
Published in 1992 by Albert Whitman & Company,
6340 Oakton Street, Morton Grove, Illinois 60053-2723.
Published simultaneously in Canada by
General Publishing, Limited, Toronto.
10 9 8 7 6 5 4 3 2 1

Library of Congress Cataloging-in-Publication Data

Nerlove, Miriam.
Purim/Miriam Nerlove.
p.   cm.
Summary: A young boy becomes caught up in
the excitement of the Purim celebration as
the rabbi relates the tale of the courageous
Queen Esther and the evil Haman.
ISBN 0-8075-6682-9
1. Purim—Juvenile literature. [1. Purim.]
I. Title.
BM695.P8N47 1992   91-19516
296.4'36—dc20   CIP
                                                           AC

Spring is coming—Purim's here!
It's time to take our costumes down.

I'm Haman—I'm a wicked man.
I wear a beard that's fuzzy brown.

My sister is Queen Esther,
with a cape and golden crown.

We go to temple after dark.
Hurry up! It's time to leave.

The rabbi will read Esther's tale
to everyone on Purim eve.

There lived in Persia long ago
a mighty king known far and wide.

This king, Ahasuerus, picked
the lovely Esther as his bride.

Haman, who advised the king,
was evil, and he hated Jews.
He plotted for them all to die
on a day that he would choose.

When Esther's uncle, Mordecai,
heard about this awful plot,
he told Queen Esther, and she planned
to have the wicked Haman caught.

Queen Esther held a lavish feast,
inviting many—Haman, too.

Then in front of all she said,
"Your Majesty, *I* am a Jew!"

"Haman, here," she told the king,
"says Jews must die—this is his plan."

The king was angry, and he said,
"The Jews will live, but kill this man!"

The Jews in Persia all rejoiced.
They thanked brave Esther on this date.

Because she ruined Haman's plan,
today we all can celebrate!

We twirl our graggers, stamp, and shout
whenever Haman's name is read.

We sing some joyful Purim songs,
And then a prayer of thanks is said.

The Purim party's starting now.
Let's all line up for our parade.

There's hamantaschen we can eat—
then contests and some games are played.

The lights are dimmed. We all sit down
to see a special Purim play.

Queen Esther's story is retold,
and when it ends, so does our day.

Purim is a holiday that takes place in spring, beginning on the fourteenth day of the Hebrew month of Adar (usually March). Jews go to the synagogue at this time to hear the story of Purim read from the Old Testament Book of Esther.

The Purim story took place in Persia around 500 B.C.E. [B.C.]. *Purim* is derived from the Hebrew word *pur,* which means "lots," and the holiday is also known as the Feast of Lots. This is because Haman, who was chief advisor to King Ahasuerus, cast lots made from small stones to determine the date on which all the Jews of Persia would be destroyed. The date chosen was the thirteenth of Adar.

Haman was an enemy of all Jews, but especially of Esther's uncle, Mordecai, who refused to bow down to Haman whenever Haman passed. Mordecai explained that Jews do not bow down to men as if to worship them. Haman was also angry because the king had honored Mordecai, who had foiled a plot to kill Ahasuerus. When he learned of Haman's plan to kill the Jews, Mordecai told Queen Esther and asked for her help.

Esther knew that only the king could save her people. But it took great courage for her to approach him. Under law, no one, not even the queen, could approach the king without being summoned. The penalty could be death. Esther fasted for three days and nights and then went before the king. He received her kindly and granted her request to hold a banquet.

At the banquet, Esther told the king of Haman's plan to kill the Jews and revealed that she herself was Jewish. She asked the king to save the Jews. The king was furious at Haman and ordered that he be hung. He then granted Esther's request by allowing the Jews to take up arms and defend themselves against soldiers whom Haman had already sent out.

On the thirteenth day of Adar, the Jews rose up and defeated Haman's soldiers. Today, Jews remember this day as the Fast of Esther.

At sundown (which marks the start of the fourteenth day of Adar), the festival and merrymaking of Purim begin with the reading of the Book of Esther in the synagogue. When Haman's name is mentioned in the Purim story, the usually quiet synagogue fills with noise. People twirl *graggers* (a type of rattle that makes a grinding sound), shout, and stamp their feet. This is done to fulfill the command in the Book of Esther, "May his name be blotted out!"

At synagogues and Jewish schools and community centers, there are plays that tell the story of Esther, carnivals, and parades. At home, Jews often have a feast, or *Purim seudah,* where triangular-shaped cookies called *hamantaschen* are served. *Shalach manot* (gifts of food and clothing) are also distributed so that all Jews can enjoy this holiday that celebrates Esther's courage and the rescue of the Jewish people from destruction.